Henry B. Wong

Teen-ager

Christ Is for You

Teen-ager

CHRIST

CONCORDIA PUBLISHING HOUSE

IS FOR YOU

By Walter Riess

SAINT LOUIS, MISSOURI

For all teen-agers who want to be
more sure
of their faith . . .
more convinced
about Jesus Christ

Markers Along the Road

Teen-ager,
Meet Your Lord!

Teen-ager, this is for you.

This is to help you find everything you ever could want. Everything — including happiness, social grace with your date, peace of mind, a creative life, a feeling of belonging, and satisfaction with yourself. And above all, Christ Himself! Think of owning Him — and all His help — for your very own!

If you're like the rest of us, you are fighting a hard battle right about now. A lot of things look like a gigantic jigsaw puzzle — your mental state, your future, your school grades, and the look of your body — and the pieces don't always want to go together.

How does a person get those pieces together, anyway?

How does a person become poised, sure of himself, able to go ahead confidently into the many doorways and hallways and backways of life?

Those are good questions.

If you stick with this booklet, we may be able to find some answers, together.

Okay?

Here we go. Jump on the wagon and stay on for a while. Let's talk — about you.

So You Can Get Along
Without God!

You may *think* you can.

You can shift for yourself. You can make your own rules and take your own chances. If you win, fine. If you lose, who cares? Not you. You don't even consider yourself that important. You don't need God — you think.

But even your thinking is done on God's gift to you — your brain.

And if you couldn't suck in that beautiful fresh oxygen through your lungs, your brain would sputter out in about four minutes.

And if you hadn't received two good legs from God at your birth, and two good arms, and muscle to move them, you couldn't even take your own chances. You couldn't even lose on your own. You couldn't even make a start.

You need God, all right.

You live on God.

Unless you can imagine that *nobody* made you — or the earth and sky and air and sea.

Old Aristotle tried to show that everything has to have a first cause. Nothing can exist without something or someone *causing* it to come into being.

11

All of which simply means that there *has* to be God. Without Him nothing makes sense at all. Even our thinking must lead us to that idea!

Besides our thinking we have our reading.

Maybe you feel that the Bible is nonsense. If you never tried to read it, you have every reason to feel that way.

It's really easy to knock a book you haven't given a chance.

But remember that you're sidetracking a book which millions of people — some of them the most brilliant minds of history — have found to be, *through experience,* living and exciting proof that God does come into the lives of people.

Would you take the word of the second president of the United States? John Adams said: "I have examined all, as well as my narrow sphere, my straitened means, and my busy life would allow me; and the result is, that the Bible is the best book in the world."

If you call the Scriptures nonsense, or shrug them off with a casual "I don't know, why bother?" you are going against the grain of nineteen centuries of human experience that the Bible is the Word of God Himself!

And if you can really ignore the Bible in your idea of getting along without God, you are ignoring what others have learned to love as the loudest witness to God's existence that there is!

So you imagine you can get away with it.

But you're an awfully lonely person. And — because you won't open yourself to the experience of God's Word — you're a terribly afraid person.

"Saul, Saul, why do you persecute Me?" Christ once asked the man who would become the greatest preacher in all history. "You hurt yourself by kicking at the goad."

"You hurt *yourself.* . . ."

And you don't have to.

In any scientific study you have to start with some basic principles. It is impossible to start with nothing. At least you have to assume that the thing you are studying — a bug, for instance — is *there,* is *real.*

Why don't you start your adventure with God by accepting the Scriptures as an honest voice about Him?

You can't get along without God. And therefore you can't get along without the one record of His work which centuries have given you — the Bible.

Go into that book like an explorer setting out to hack through the jungles of Brazil, or like a mathematician determined to find the answer to a puzzling equation. Get yourself a different translation, like the Revised Standard Version or Moffatt, or even a paraphrase like Phillips, and compare, and *search* for yourself!

You'll find, all right.

You'll find God waiting to tap you on the shoulder and to whisper into your ear some of the most dazzling bits of information you've ever heard.

"And this is eternal life, to know You, the only true God, and Jesus Christ, whom You have sent."

You're Too Small
for God to Notice

Did you ever have the chance to take an airliner and to look down over a city stretching flat and quiet beneath you?

From your plane you can't see a single human being. Now and then a cloud will blot out whole miles of buildings. From the air you cannot find your home, not even your neighborhood. Everything floats together in one hazy picture of smoke, air, and civilization.

Almost any time you see this, the thought will strike you: *How small I am down there among all those buildings!*

And then you think of God, seeing the whole world in one glance, looking over the entire earth with one sweep of His eye. How small you must look to Him! If He can even find you — if He can even try to spot you — if He even cares!

You can't believe He does care. It's impossible to believe that. For if He cares for you, then He must care as much for each individual Chinese of all the millions and millions of Chinese on the globe. And He must care as much for all the Europeans, for all the Japanese and Indians. No one could have so much

15

attention in him to care for every single one of those people!

That stands to reason. And it also stands to reason that God, then, must care for hardly anybody. He probably just lets the world go on and lets all the people get into scrapes by themselves and kill one another off without batting an eyelash. Maybe He made the first one or two people. But that's where His care ended.

You're right. All that — every bit of it — stands to reason!

There's only one thing wrong with it: *God* doesn't stand to reason.

You can put down on paper a drawing to illustrate Euclid's geometry: you can wrap up the atom bomb in a formula; you can describe the circumference of the earth with a few letters and numbers. But you simply cannot — no matter how hard you try — you simply *cannot* make God fit your reason. And its limits!

What about God fits reason? Can you reason out the birth of Christ from a virgin mother? Or the strange love which God held for all men — that He even went so far as to send Jesus Christ, His Son, to get the people of the earth back to Him? And all that after they had slapped His face and told Him plenty of times, in a million different hideous ways, that they hated Him and wanted no part of Him?

Can you figure God loving Noah so much that He saved this one man and his family while all the God-hating people of the earth died in the Flood? Why didn't the Lord do the job right and finish us all off and let it go at that? Always that second chance!

16

Always that extra bit of love! Always that smile after being cursed, scorned. What a God! What a Savior!

Truly, now, would you want any other kind? Would you want a god you could put between your hands and hold in front of you, saying "Now I've got you!"

That's the kind of god a lot of folks of all ages have wanted. Worse, they made that kind of god. Little and big images of wood, stone, brass, marble, and even jewels, began popping up all around the world not long after the real God made it.

Those people were only kidding themselves. They kidded themselves right into hell. A hell without the real God around, ever.

What all of us really want is a God above our highest dreams — Someone so far above us that all our life we will be stretching just to touch Him — yet Someone so close that we will know He is with us all the time. That kind of God will notice us. Because that kind of God makes His home *inside* of us.

"Christ," said the Apostle Paul — "Christ is in you."

Don't try to figure that one out, either. You won't get very far.

Just turn to yourself, put this book down for a moment, and try to determine if Christ has come into you by faith.

Do you think He loves you?

Do you think He died for you?

Do you love others — because He died for them, too?

Do you know He pays attention to your everyday life?

17

Do you forgive others even after they've hurt you — simply because you know He has forgiven you — everything?

Answer *yes!* He gives Himself to you — as your own personal Savior. As big as the heavens — yet right in you.

You Think
God Kills Fun?

Somehow you've maybe thought of God as a huge man sitting on a great oak throne, white beard reaching to His knees, a solemn scowl on His face — threatening to smash down with His rod anyone who steps out of line and laughs in church.

Funny how some people get that kind of idea about God. Where did the notion come from in the first place?

Not from Scripture! On the contrary one of the psalms actually challenges us to "taste and see that the Lord is *good.*"

Not from the lives of Christians who know Christ intimately. These folks can afford to have the best sense of humor around. Their future is in the hands of their Lord and Master. They look forward to an eternity of happiness. They always know that everything is right. They don't have to worry. *They really can smile.*

So who gave birth to this idea that God kills fun?

That's right. Again — the people who never really came to *know* God.

You know, the ones who shake their heads at the

folks who go to church Sundays. The ones who simply can't understand "what the suckers see in that racket."

These are the critics who have painted God to the rest of the world as an old man who smothers enjoyment of life.

Christian teen-agers, especially, who have accepted Christ as their Lord and Savior, as the Son of God whom God gave to us, would be surprised to know that God kills fun.

Ever go out with a gang from a Christian church?

If anything, Christian teen-agers can have a whale of a better time than anyone else. Because their God doesn't loom over them like a giant with a whip.

Their God has revealed Himself in Christ!

And what a wonderful Person is Christ!

You can't know Him without loving Him — all the way. The Christ who brought a teen-age daughter of Jairus back to life, who took the children of Palestine on His knee, who lashed out at the show-off Pharisees standing on street corners and praying in a loud voice, who finally went the whole distance for us and died, who rose and went to heaven to keep a place open for you and me. . . .

This Christ can be ours.

Christian teen-agers have Him!

You think they don't know it? You think this is just book knowledge? You think they don't feel Him near them?

You think Christ Himself doesn't *send* fun? He *is* fun — in a wonderful sort of way!

It's a wonderful, refreshing adventure to go through a single day with Christ at your elbow.

That's why Christian teen-agers laugh longer and

louder, play harder, work better, get along with one another, and lead others in the really happy life.

Until you become better acquainted with Christ, you simply can't know what God is really like. Any more than an unborn child can know what his mother looks like.

That's exactly how the Bible talks about those of us who have not accepted Christ as our Whole Love for life — it calls us "unborn."

Christ Himself told people: "You have to be born *again*."

He meant that they had to go through a spiritual birth *after* their physical birth. Otherwise they wouldn't know what life was really all about.

Now, do you want to call Christ a kill-joy before you've tried His way?

Would you judge a person who came up to you before giving him a chance to be your friend?

If you did judge such a person, would *he* be the fool, or would *you*?

Next time you run into a pal who knows Christ, really ask yourself: "Is she bored or dull?" "Is he a dead stick?"

"Or am *I* missing something — and Someone?"

You Think God Ought to Run the World Better

Sure, there's the draft. And then the stories of how an H-bomb attack by Russia could wipe out the whole country.

It's really hard to plan anything in this kind of world. Instead of just going out for a job after high school, you've got to go into the Armed Services, and that's no picnic. You have to push off everything you've planned and dreamed until Uncle Sam or another Uncle somewhere behind the Iron Curtain decides to let you alone. If you're a girl, you've got to wait, and wait some more. If you're a young man, you've got to wait. . . .

When a bunch of dictators and a few war lords can boss the rest of the world and make a million others wait on them, it doesn't seem to make sense to talk about God ruling the world. Maybe He created it, but He sure let it get messed up. Christians look awfully funny praying to God when Uncle Peter Shrevnetzky in Lower Slatternia can stir up such a brew of trouble for Joe Doakes in the United States.

Well, the Christians may look funny. They won't

deny that. But if you let them explain, they may have something on their side, too.

They won't deny the world's in a mess. They won't deny that Uncle Peter Shrevnetzky's got a lot more power than any man should have. Or that the hydrogen bomb makes a mighty big scare.

But who put Uncle Peter where he is — on the throne of Slatternia? And who worked night and day to design and put together the H-bomb? Whose fault is it that we have to read, with our morning breakfast, a newspaper chuck full of threats?

Is that God's fault?

Not on your life.

When God made that first person, far back in history's early shadows, He did a pretty fine job. That first person did not act like Uncle Peter Shrevnetzky. He was not interested in making H-bombs, or even in throwing rocks at monkeys. That first person — believe it or not — was *good*, clear through *good*.

Now if he'd have only stayed that way — this man Adam — there would be no Uncle Peters today, and no draft. But he didn't. Adam got sick. He got deathly sick.

He went against God, following the lead of that first woman, his wife Eve. And that was that.

Uncle Peter, Hitler, Mussolini, and all the men who would like to toss an H-bomb, are direct descendants of the sick Adam and the sick Eve. The same Adam and the same Eve who pushed God away because they wanted to up their own stock.

But there's another something to add to this tragedy. And it means a lot as far as Uncle Peter — and you, too — are concerned.

26

God didn't let Adam and Eve alone after they took sick with their revolt against Him. God ran after them. Jesus Christ, God, chased them through history until He got them to see that He had forgiven them. Would you believe it?

Jesus Christ did not let the world alone!

In fact, "God loved the world so dearly that He gave His only Son, so that everyone who believes in Him may have eternal life, instead of perishing. . . ."

Get those two words, *"eternal life"!* They mean just what they say — *no death.*

Even in the face of the H-bomb. Because we're not talking about physical death. Everybody goes through that. Or almost everybody.

But all physical death really amounts to is a hallway into eternity. It's only a swinging door that ushers us — sometimes against our will — into the visible presence of Jesus Christ.

And that's where the issues of life and death are really settled, right across the table. That's where even Christians really get to know what eternal life can mean.

But eternal life actually starts right here. Christians know that, too. Physical death has no meaning at all when you know you will be with Christ forever, wonderfully alive, breathing in the clear, sparkling air of heaven with Him. Then physical death comes as a gift from the sky. The hallway is wonderfully lighted and mirrored.

No, sir, Christ never lets us alone — those of us who tell Him we believe, and we love Him. We can always be sure that He wants us, and wants us badly.

27

And then we can also be sure that He wants the rest of the world, and wants it just as much. He wants even Uncle Peter Shrevnetzky, so anxious to play with his little bombs. He wants everybody on every continent to find eternal life in Him.

As long as this world stands, Christ's offer will stay open. He promises to give men mercy until the final Day of Judgment.

Well, then, how long *will* the world stand?

Here Uncle Peter Shrevnetzky, far behind the Iron Curtain, seems to hold all the aces. He can push the tiny red button in the right drawer of his black walnut desk and send us all into oblivion. He can bark an order to an aide and shoot hundreds of intercontinental ballistic missiles into the sky, headed directly for you and me. Just a button, just an order, and the world blows up beneath us. Right?

Wrong.

Because Christ not only offers everyone — even Uncle Peter — His love and forgiveness. Christ also rules Uncle Peter, whether Uncle Peter likes it or not. Christ rules *all things,* says the Bible, by the Word of His power. It is Christ who guides Uncle Peter's hand. It is Christ who created the air on which those intercontinental bombers fly — and who can, if He will, take that air away from the bombers in a second. It is Christ — always, always Christ — who rules and still rules when the dictators crow the loudest.

Do you believe this?

It's one of those matters which you simply must take on faith, since Christ will not be visible until He comes again to earth — as He has, by the way, pledged to do. Christ will not tap you on the arm, turn you

28

around, make Himself visible to you now so that you can see Him at work ruling the world and all its Uncle Peters. Christ expects faith, and even demands it, from those who want His help.

But that faith can come to you. And when it does, you won't worry about Uncle Peter or the H-bomb. You won't have to — because you will know who butters your bread and at the same time watches Uncle Peter's nervous hands. "This is the victory which overcomes the world, even our faith."

God runs the world, all right. He runs it the way He wants to run it. Just listen close enough, and you'll hear the rustle of His cloak even in the back rooms of Washington, or at the long tables of the UN, and behind the gloomy turrets of the Kremlin.

And all He says to you is this: *Only believe.*

You Can't Believe
Those Bible "Fairy Tales"

For instance, that the world was created in six days.

— Or that a flood really covered the whole earth.

— Or that Moses made water come out of a rock in the desert.

— Or that Peter healed the dying. . . .

Did you ever take a look at yourself? No, I mean a real good long look — in a mirror about six feet high and three feet wide?

What did you see?

That's easy. Two eyes, two ears, a nose, a mouth, a torso, or a trunk, two legs, two feet (if the mirror was big enough), and maybe a grin to boot. You saw you — a person, a young man or a young lady, equipped with the usual equipment.

"*Usual*" equipment, because everyone has it — or almost everyone!

How long did it take for you to get that "usual" equipment?

You know the facts of life. Nine months, more

or less, you were in your mother before birth. Nine months.

Are you really saying that you got that magnificent machine called your body in nine short months?

Your system of nerves, so complicated that a mile of delicate "brain" machines could not duplicate it, your eyesight, your balance, your emotional makeup — could these really grow by themselves out of nothingness in nine months?

Take another look in that mirror, and ask yourself if *you* aren't one of God's miracles?

You doubt that an angel ever appeared to Mary. But how can you doubt, after searching yourself through and through and never getting to the bottom of the wonders in your own body and mind, that the Lord Himself had a lot to do with your creation?

You fall in love with that fellow or girl. What does this "falling in love" mean to you? Chemicals in action and reaction? Animal desire and animal fulfillment? Or is there just a touch of miracle in your love for that other person? Has something — and Someone — far beyond and above you given you an emotion you never had a right to expect: a feeling very near the divine? Has a miracle touched your life here, too?

You're not the only one who lives to doubt the Bible's miracles. Could it be that you doubt the Bible's miracles simply because you don't see the miracles in your own life, which loom up right in front of your eyes? Many good scientists stand among the best Christians, because they see behind the vast beautiful pattern of life and life's functions the certain hand of God. Miracles are with us — even if we don't always see them.

Miracles go on constantly outside of us, too. A few years ago people would have called you a crackpot if you had told them about laser beams, space travel, or communication by satellite. Splitting the atom was once proclaimed, even by some scientists, an impossible feat. And many people even in the church felt such a thing could never happen because "the age of miracles is over."

Is it? Is it really?

Are the miracles of the Bible really so fantastic, so unbelievable, in the light of our modern wonders?

What would Noah have said if you had shown him a drawing of today's rockets? What would Peter have said if you had shown him a photo of a modern preacher reaching millions in one televised half hour? They probably would have shaken their heads and said: "Only the Lord could do *that!*"

And, of course, they would have been perfectly right.

Because even our modern miracles are a gift of the same God and Savior who gave us the Bible. The same Lord who sent the Flood sent us men and brains equipped to invent the electric light, to build and fly an airplane, to plan a rocket trip to outer space. And if you don't want to believe the miracles of the Bible, when God dealt so directly with men, then you ought to deny the miracles which He has given to us today — even though they do not come so directly as those in Scripture.

If, after thinking it all over, you accept miracles, you accept yourself. For — under God — you yourself are a walking, living miracle. In your body you own a miraculous instrument for doing. In your mind you own a miraculous instrument for thinking, planning, inventing, creating.

You are God's creation. You are the one for whom Christ offered Himself. In all that you are a miracle and more than a miracle. You were really a part of God's eternal plan when He made this earth.

Think of that the next time you read your Bible. God *did* make man out of clay. He *did* show Israel the way out of the desert with a cloud and a fire. Jesus Christ *did* raise Lazarus from the dead. His disciples *did* heal the sick and the maimed. And all of us someday *will* see our Lord face to face in the life after life.

Is it so hard for you to believe? Take another look . . . just for a moment . . . at the miracle of your own self. The same God who made you reigns today over all nature, over all the world. Our Lord can still change His universe, as a sculptor molds his creation.

Sure, miracles still happen. Miracles will always happen. Because God is God. And you are not really your own, but *His*.

So You Don't Want to Become a Namby-Pamby Christian

Who does?

Have you fallen for the old line that says a heart-and-soul Christian walks around in a heavenly trance, a lily in one hand, a Bible in the other, and a glow in his pale face — preaching at everyone he meets that heaven is the only place which really counts?

If you have, guess again.

Take a good long look at that husky Martin Luther, standing up before the Emperor and the Diet at the town of Worms, threatened with death and dishonor . . . yet staying firm and daring the power of an empire to make him take back the Truth!

Or go back even farther, to that day when Paul was taken out of the city, stoned until he looked dead, because he dared to talk Christ, and left alone. Then watch him. He gets to his feet, dazedly, tries to walk, keeps taking one bleeding step after another — and goes on talking Christ to a world without God!

You call that "namby-pamby"?

Or see those first Christians, told they would be eaten by lions if they did not deny Christ — yet going for His sake right into the arena, and singing songs while the starved animals charged!

If that kind of courage is "goody-goody," we could use a lot more of it in *our* battles, couldn't we?

Actually it is just about as hard for a real Christian to be "goody-goody" as it is for a toy steam shovel to clear the Panama Canal. Christians — real Christians — have a fight on their hands. They have a calling and a challenge. And they don't back down from it or retreat into a lily-white pious attitude. They fight.

They fight wrong. They fight injustice. They fight slavery of every kind. They fight hate. They fight Satan.

Even more important, real Christians fight *for* something.

They know that their God lives — that He is real, and that He stands with them. So they stand up for Him. They work to defend Him against every form of slander or slur. They try hard to tell the world He is God — that He came into the world as Christ, to save those who believe in Him from their own self-made destruction. They labor to see the name of *Christ* ring from every mike and TV set, from flags and loud-speakers, from lips and hearts everywhere which know His presence.

People who do not know Christ at all, who have never offered themselves to Him, are the first to call Christians silly little names. This is a favorite trick of cowardice. It is the same kind of trick that Goebbels used in deceiving the people of Germany into following Hitler before and during World War II. We call it the "Big Smear."

Once you do come to know Christ personally — friend to Friend — once you do feel His constant pres-

38

ence with you, once you do take up your cross to follow Him, exciting things happen to you.

Every "ordinary" minute grows thrilling in its adventure. You've heard how "falling in love" changes life. Maybe you know that from personal experience. Well, falling in love with Jesus Christ is not different. It is even more of an adventure. Once you know Him as yours, every tree seems to be singing a psalm to Him — every pup with wagging tail seems happy because Christ lives — and every waterfall seems to want to burble its joy because Christ has become yours. "All things have become new for me!" cried Paul.

Temptations which once dragged you down now become easy to master. You don't need drink, you don't need nicotine. You can take them or leave them. You have "this one Treasure" — and around that Treasure, Christ, you arrange your whole life. Everything falls into place for the first time. Big items shrink to little concerns. And once tiny matters sprout into importance.

Suddenly you are strong. You feel the power of God Himself undergirding your decisions, your efforts, your work. A winner of the National Open golf tournament said it in front of the microphones: "I thank God for His help — He gave me unbelievable power." A UCLA All-American fullback chose for his motto Psalm 18:29: "For by Thee I have run through a troop, and by my God have I leaped over a wall."

And he lived it.

You may be stronger than you think.

But Don't Christians Say
That Sex Is Wrong?

You might as well ask, "Do weathermen say that storms are bad?"

Well, *are* storms bad?

Suppose, on a summer day, a mass of dark-gray clouds swoops in low over your home, opens up and pours out an inch or so of gorgeous rain on your garden. You call that a storm. Is it bad?

But suppose, on that same summer day, a blistering maze of yellow streamers comes rolling down at you, spin themselves into a dither, and tear the roof off your house. You call that a storm, too, don't you? Is it bad? Silly question!

No, Christians do not say that sex is wrong. But they do say that sex is wrong *when it's used wrong*. When it hits, like the bad storm, at the wrong time and the wrong place.

You go on a date with someone you really like a lot. After the movie you stop for a hamburger and coke and drive on. You park. Something happens. You lose your controls, and pretty soon you're petting in a way that you never thought you could. Even *you* are scared of you then. Because you know downright well you aren't doing this because you want to, but because you've been trapped into doing it by a little monster inside of you that's running hog-wild!

What kind of storm would you call that?

Storms that get out of control, that sweep their way through every obstacle they meet, are just plain bad storms. To anybody. It's not different with sexual storms.

"Sexual freedom," you hear people say. "That's fun. That's for me." But these people are the last to know what sexual freedom is. Because if you could get into their minds and see how tormented they are by sexual desires night and day, morning and noon and evening, you would call them slaves. Slaves to the passions that have grown into tornadoes way out of control. Slaves to themselves. Sure, they prate about sexual freedom. It's a way to excuse sexual slavery.

Christians don't like slavery — of any kind. Christ said: "I am the Way, the Truth, and the Life . . . and the Truth shall make you *free.*"

That kind of freedom is real.

But don't let anyone kid you, it takes a fight. It takes a real young man, and a real young lady, to battle off the tremendous draw of sex *at the wrong time,* in the wrong place. Look at the fight the Apostle Paul himself had to put up. "Do you remember," he asks you, "how on a racing track every competitor runs, but only one wins the prize? Well, you ought to run with your minds fixed on winning the prize!" Every competitor in athletic events goes into serious training. Athletes will take tremendous pains — for a fading crown of leaves. But our contest is for an eternal crown that will never fade.

42

"I run the race, then, with determination. I am no shadow-boxer, I really fight! I am my body's sternest master. . . !"

Well, what does all this mean? Does it mean you should keep away from sex entirely, never, never hold hands with your girl, never kiss her, never hope or plan to marry. . . ?

There are some folks who think that way. But, you see, they're putting themselves into slavery in the *other direction*. They have become slaves to their fears of sex and to their own false ideas about the purpose of sex.

It's a lot harder to use sex rightly than it is to either let it boss you or let it scare you! You don't master sex by running away from it any more than you master it by giving in to it every time it wags a finger at you.

Say you are a young man. You really like your girl. She thinks and talks your language. When you're out on a date together, you fit like two pieces in a jigsaw puzzle. When you worship together, you mean it — both of you. You make sense together, and you know it, and your friends know it. You like this girl so much you'd like to make it a habit to be with her. You can even see the time when you and she will hit it off regularly and join hands at the altar. . . .

In that case you'd be silly not to express your love, not to continue enjoying life together with her through dates, outings, get-togethers with others of your own age and faith. *As long as you sincerely respect her, and live up to your respect.* As long as your expression of love doesn't sink into a "passion pit" kind of thing that makes a game of sex, which never in itself equals love!

Now, would you want to go farther than love with respect — honestly? If you really like this girl, really even *love* her, would you want to load her and your conscience and life down with worries and guilt? You take no chances — but she does. Playing too far with sex can ruin her life, her family, her future, her body. You know that, don't you?

— You have thought about your Lord long enough to know that He has come into your body, and into the body of your girl friend. "Have you forgotten," asks Paul, "that your body is the temple of the Holy Spirit, who lives in you, and that you are not the owner of your own body? You have been bought, and at what a price!" (1 Corinthians 6:19, *Phillips.*) No, you haven't forgotten that fact — how precious the Lord has made you by coming into you.

Neither you nor your girl would want to do anything to maim your Lord's work. It all adds up to something like this: The more you love your girl, the more you'll stay away from things that hurt her body, her temple in which the Holy Spirit Himself lives.

And when you *do* marry, you'll find out that sex means a lot more than just fun or excitement. Sex is all wrapped up with God's way of creating people — more temples for His presence.

When you take your first look at your first baby, someday — whether you're a young man or a young lady — you'll be mighty glad you handled sex with respect and used it with love.

You Want Something
to Live By That Works

Everyone on God's earth has an idea on this subject. Doctors, psychiatrists, scientists, shoemakers, philosophers, machinists — all of them will tell you, at the drop of a hat, one formula or another for getting along in life.

"Now, here," they will say, "is something that really *works!*" Then, usually, you're in for it — a long, long play-back on how to be happy for a quarter. Read this book, take this pill, go to this movie, and you're all set. You've had it, brother.

You sure have.

Let's start right off by agreeing that no one ordinary book, no single pill, no one easy way out, will do the trick of carrying us through life on wings of song. In the first place, who says we were made to go through life on wings of song? In the second place, would we want to if we could? Don't you doubt it? I do.

We may kid ourselves that we would like to glide through all our days on a solid gold feather, but how long would we like that kind of life if we had it? The divorce rate and suicide rate rank just as high, or higher, than ordinary among those who "have it made." Evidently the plush coach ride is not even close to an answer.

What do we really want out of life? Maybe that's the question we have to answer before we can discover what will work to get us what we want!

Well, what do *you* want?

What would it take to make *you* really happy?

A psychologist who helps advertisers win customers says that every one of us spends his life trying to get these four things:

> **sustenance**
>
> **sex**
>
> **security**
>
> **status**

Which means that unless we have all four — food and drink, romantic love affairs, secure future, and a position among our people, we just won't feel happy or complete.

Probably our friend the psychologist knows what he's talking about. Certainly life is made up of a number of things. And you could practically fit all of life into those four words listed above.

But one question: After you've won them all, would you *then* be happy, really content?

That's the $64,000 question.

Put yourself in this position for a moment. After 40 years of work and living you've got a job as head buyer in a large city department store. You have married and have a fine family of three children — two girls and a boy. You are in perfect health and carry every form of insurance, including sick benefits in case you should have to miss work. You could get involved in an auto accident tomorrow and still collect your paycheck for the rest of your life. Your neighbors and friends look up to you as a leader in the community; you appear at all the right places, say the right words, and make the right gestures.

Would having all this work for you? Would you be really happy? Do you think so?

Chances are that some night, after some party with your crowd, you'd come home, sit on your bed, look at everything you have and are, and wonder just what it all amounts to.

And suddenly you'd realize you were missing something. There would be a big hollow somewhere in your heart. You would not be able to locate it. You wouldn't begin to point to it. You would only know something very important was lacking — something necessary to make life happy for you.

That "something" is God.

Look again at those four words: sustenance, sex, security, status. They all deal with *human* values, don't they?

And those four words, with no more added, also deal with *animal* values. What else does a dog, for instance, want besides food, sex, a place to live, and a dominating position over other animals?

You can't believe, can you, that you would be satisfied with the same things that satisfy animals! Certainly not!

Deep inside of you, you realize that God made you. From what you see all around you, you can't help knowing there is a God. Even more certain than that, you feel a hunger for God's power. You don't know how, really, to get along without Him.

No sustenance, sex, security, or status will take care of that need in you. Because you are not an animal. You are God's creature, made for Him, to have Him with you as your Savior and King.

That works.

Don't rest until you have it. It's the one thing in life worth going for all the way.

Just kneel down, alone, and pray: Lord Jesus Christ, give me Yourself.

And wait.

You're Clumsy and Awkward and Can't Help It?

You may be clumsy and awkward. But don't be too sure you can't help it.

Did you ever watch a young colt frisking in the pasture — stiff legs, thin body, narrow neck, bulging eyes, all racing in every direction in one single motion?

That colt is growing up. Like you . . . in your teens. When bones and muscles grow, they don't grow in perfect harmony. One speeds, another part crawls. Result — this works well, that doesn't. Co-ordination isn't always there.

For that reason not all of us can be the heroes of the basketball court or the football field, or even of the high school gym class — not even if we tried. Not, anyway, until all our differing bones and muscles hit the end of the growing trail.

Nevertheless that's not the whole of it. Maybe you won't ever be a pro football star or head of your high school cheering section or even a good ping-pong artist.

But you *can* add a certain "grace" to your everyday actions!

A lot of us walk through our homes and high

schools with head bent down, shoulders slouching, feet shuffling, clothing sagging, hair uncombed and eyes tired. We're tired. We have nothing great to hope for. We aren't excited about anything, and we don't care who knows it. Frankly, we're bored stiff with the whole business.

To put it lightly, we look "ungraceful." To put it more realistically, we look like a hawk in a canary cage. We don't fit. We don't belong to the scene around us.

But why is this? Is the reason inside our limbs? Hardly that. We can get along. We're average. We might not be world-beaters on the gym floor, but we can move around. What's happened to us that we have to lope through our high school and home like a Sad Sack on crutches?

For the answer to that you might have to go into the relation of mind to body.

Your doctor will tell you that your body reacts to your mental condition. If you are depressed mentally, your posture slips into a big ? instead of an !. If you are "down" in your mind, you growl at people. You move in jerks and talk in jerks. You miss your social chances.

In other words, the state of your mind helps to control the grace of your body — the way that you move, talk to others, and *act*, alone and publicly. If you feel rough inside, you will act rough on the outside. And others will see that you are acting that way.

What can be done about this situation? Suppose you feel clumsy inside and can't help it, can't fight it, and finally just have to give in to that feeling?

A high school girl in Detroit told of the most

wonderful experience in her life. During an English period she suddenly came down with a headache that seemed to throb down into her brain. She could barely stand it. She hurried to the nurse's office, only to find it locked. She walked away, and finally sat down to rest on the couch in the rest room. And there it dawned on her that she could carry through what she had learned in long hours with her Bible.

She could pray.

Alone, she put her face to the wall and very simply asked God to take away her headache. She said later that her prayer was very ungainly, not at all well worded. But she did manage to get it out — and to leave it all up to God to answer in His own way: *Yes, No,* or just, *Wait.*

That she was answered with a *Yes* should not, perhaps, have surprised her as greatly as it did. Nor should it surprise us. If the stories about Christ healing people blind, deaf, sick to death, are true, and if Christ is God to this very day, then He cannot be any less the Healer than He was in the days which the New Testament describes! And if He is still that same Healer, then we would be foolish not to ask Him to give us the grace that we need to be happy and well with everyone around us!

"You don't have," St. James said, "because you don't ask!"

If you want to do something to help your state of mind and your state of body,

"*Ask,* and it shall be given to you."

Ask in the name of Jesus Christ and believe. And you will have started on the road to being graceful — inside and out.

You Don't Know How
to Find Your Real Job

One of the biggest questions high schoolers have to face is this: *What am I going to do with myself?*

If you go down to an employment office, you'll see hundreds of jobs lined up for men and women. Most of those jobs take some kind of training; you can't just jump in and do them without learning something about them.

In other words, you should start thinking about the kind of work you're going to do later. And more than that — you sure would be smart to take special training along the way in preparation for getting the job you're most suited for by nature, and the job you're going to handle the best.

Now comes the corker. How can you understand yourself well enough **now** to choose your job **for life?** What are the chances you'll make a blunder? What if you do? Can you switch later on without harming yourself?

Naturally you don't want to make a mistake. Training for a job takes years of your life, even in high school. Training for the wrong job means wasted years, in a sense. And any kind of waste of precious human life is silly, isn't it? Especially when that life is your own!

So you want to settle down to this thing as seriously as you can. This is an important decision, and you want to do everything possible to make it the right decision.

Okay?

With that in mind, let's note down some possibilities.

First, you can go to a counselor, either in your high school or elsewhere, who will probably give you two things:

1) an aptitude test

2) advice based on that test.

It's really amazing how few high school students like yourself ever take advantage of the counseling service offered by their school and community! It's more than amazing. It's almost tragic. Because high school counselors possess aptitude exams and other devices which can help you a lot in finding what you are cut out to do.

Second, you can do some reading of your own. Your public library has books which deal with choice of vocation. All you have to do is walk up to the girl at the desk, mention vocation, and you'll probably get enough printed material to keep you reading into the night.

You take these books home, read them through (the ones you can get through), and think until you can't think any more. The best of these books give you small self-tests, which will help reveal to you just what *you* are all about. The worst of them overwhelm you with page after page of statistics about your I. Q., the I. Q. of the nation and the world, and then leave you hanging in thin air with nothing to hold to but a few cloudy tables. Maybe you have an idea of your job; maybe you don't.

Then there's the philosopher's technique of simply sitting down to think through the whole business on your own. You choose a comfortable chair, preferably by a smoking fireplace, turn down the light, and drift off into dreaming about yourself. You look into your past — the first imaginations which you had about yourself, those first clear dreams of what you wanted to become. Even if those dreams changed from day to day, or even hour to hour, they were real enough. They did something to you. Maybe you can find yourself in them. Maybe you ought to become the airline pilot you envisioned you would be someday. Maybe you ought to enter modeling school and try to make that early idea a reality now. . . .

Or possibly you could make use of all these techniques to learn where you belong in the workaday world. What would you decide to do after:

> visiting a counselor
> taking an aptitude test
> reading vocational books
> thinking and dreaming about your past ideas?

Really, now, where do you think all these roads would lead you?

To a dozen different destinations, maybe?

Then add the advice you'll get — from your parents, who want to help you. From your pastor, from your friends, who want to stand with you. From your special girl or boy friend, who may have a unique interest in your future work. There it comes — oodles of advice, floating at you from every direction of your own private universe. And probably every piece of advice differs in some way from the others.

By now you realize you'll have to figure your own way through this problem. You're grateful for all the help you've received. You love your parents and friends and what they've done to guide. But, in the last analysis, the decision will have to be yours — yours, and no one else's!

Well, after you've gathered together all the advice and suggestions which your parents, high school, pastor, and friends can offer you, is there any way to be sure that the road you finally pick is the right road? How can you get that assurance?

There is only one way.

If you have decided to commit your way to Christ's will, you'll find the right job. It may take time, but through experience God will lead you to your right work. Believe that. And more than that — look at what the very first psalm in Scripture has to say about the Christian: ". . . **whatever** he does, he prospers!"

Since the Lord Himself made you, and made you for a purpose hidden with Him, the only way you can really fulfill your life's mission is to make sure that His will is done in your life.

How can you do that? Simple.

You have to give yourself to Him — completely, without reservation, through a prayer of commitment and constant study of the Scriptures. You have to lose yourself in God, and so find yourself.

Once you've made that decision for Christ to lead your life all the way, every right thing you do seems more filled with purpose. And every right thing you do becomes more successful . . . because He is guiding it and blessing it.

You Find It Hard
to Make Friends

Pal John stands in front of the bathroom mirror, brushing his hair until it glistens. He knots his tie in a big Beau Brummel, hunches up his jacket, squints, and leaves for his big date.

Or take our gal Milly, who can't get enough of cosmetics. She's blown over $7.50 this last month for the latest shades of lipstick, and she isn't satisfied tonight that her pick was just right. She plans to do some more baby-sitting, and then some more spending, and will sure-as-you-go get really pretty that way — she thinks.

John and Milly aren't exactly exceptions. They feel that the secret to popularity is looking right. The latest fashions out of *Seventeen* to make "that simply gorgeous figure" — or that nasty swirl of hair on the top of John's skull, designed to "wow the girls" — or a natty twist of the neckline to create "that come-hither look" — these are tricks of the trade. Every magazine on the rack tries to sell them to us. You can be popular if . . . you buy the right dress, jacket, perfume, car, skates, cigarets, lipstick, deodorant, dogfood, etc., etc.

John and Milly may get to be popular, too. But they won't have the haircomb or the cosmetics kit to thank for it. Underneath John and Milly may be just the kind of people whom others like, and they'll make friends *in spite of the ads,* not because of them. And all the while John and Milly will be ignorant of the real way to get and stay tops with people they like.

Because getting — getting anything, even a good pat of lipstick or a pair of stuffed shoulders — doesn't win friends. Attracting attention does not make friends. Calling for admiration through a show of talents does not make friends in spite of the promises of piano and harmonica manufacturers. You don't get popular by brushing with this toothpaste or smoking this filter brand or joining the girls' Gown-of-the-Month Sewing Club. Of course, if the advertisers convince you of the fact that their product will give you automatic popularity, you'll buy — and they'll be the richer for it. But you won't be any wiser for it nor any more popular in the real sense of the word.

You see, the real secret of popularity can be summed up in two tiny phrases:

      a) liking others

      b) giving yourself to others.

You've met that fellow or girl who just naturally has the crowd swirling around. What does it? It's simply the fact that the popular person likes people and is trying to add to the enjoyment of those people.

Real popularity comes hard. Because it means self-denial. It means giving in to the wishes of others. Notice how quick the crowd leaves the fellow who always wants to have his own way about things. Note how the girls ditch Pearl when she constantly brags about her dates at the youth meetings. But watch

64

how high that fellow rates who does what the crowd wants to do — and always seems to love it!

How much Jesus talked about self-denial! Most people think He meant skipping food and fun. Nonsense. He meant *conquering yourself* — pushing yourself down so that other people — and He Himself! — could get on top in your life. This is not only the secret to popularity. This is the secret of happiness in life. This is one of the keynotes of the life in Christ.

Come to think about it, you'll find popularity coming a lot easier after you've found Christ, and after you've offered yourself body and soul to Him. Then it won't be hard to give yourself to others. Because, knowing that Christ loves them *too*, you'll go all the way to liking them — and to squelching your own desires to satisfy the needs and wants of others.

Try it sometime. Love Christ, love others, and *give*.

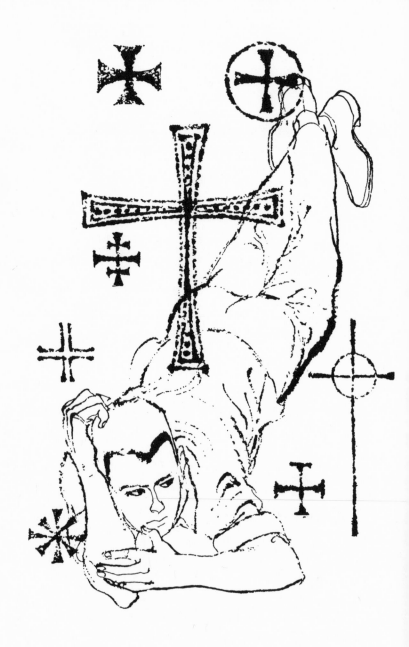

All the Church Does
Is Shout Laws

And "the church" wants to stuff them down your throat over TV, radio, and even through the movies — like a great big word machine running on perpetual motion.

There are the evangelists who claim to heal, and there are the preachers who climb the mike, and the arm-wavers who cry at you to get into church or you will die, or something. And every preacher and every organization which sends out a preacher has a program which takes your money and your time — all of both that you're willing to give.

And then the laws!

Fifteen hundred of them at least — laws about drinking, smoking, dancing, parties, coming in late or getting up late, cursing, swearing, marrying, burying — teachings about Baptism and Holy Communion and confirmation and long-sounding words like sanctification, justification, immersion, transubstantiation, and sin.

By this time you've been thrown for a loss back on your own 10-yard-line. You shiver every time you look at a steeple. You want to live your own life without any church standing over you and shouting

67

orders. But still you get a guilty tinge every step you take past that bulletin board on the corner — the one that says: "Welcome, Next Sunday!"

Even if you decide to get full-force behind a church, you wouldn't know for a moment how to choose from among the large variety of small and large, sweet and sour, quiet and loud groups that claim to be the one and only true church of Christ in the world. Every church seems so sure that it holds the keys to the kingdom of heaven itself. Where do you start when you want to choose the *right* church?

Now stick with us while we nail down a fact which a lot of us ignore. *There is really only one church,* believe it or not — in spite of all the hundreds of "churches" which advertise themselves loudly and clearly in our ears!

When Christ was on earth visibly, He started the church. He started the church with people who believed in Him — that He was God revealed, that He had come to save them for an eternity in heaven. He started the church with people who loved Him — loved Him enough to die for Him rather than leave Him.

God told about the coming of Jesus Christ, His life and death, why He had to die, and the meaning of His resurrection and ascension, through the writings of prophets, poets, historians — and even letter writers like St. Paul. Students of Scripture have studied these writings for centuries to gather the Bible's teachings together, always keeping Christ at the center of them. That, for instance, is what Martin Luther did when he wrote his catechisms. Such books contain nothing else but the teachings of Christ in Scripture.

68

Besides the right teachings, Christ gave us, when He was on earth visibly, certain ways to tell which people were really in His church. "By this," He said, "everyone will know that you are My disciples — that you love one another." Naturally, anyone who says he belongs to the true church and yet persists in undercutting you or anyone else, had better do a good deal of self-searching.

Another hint of Christ about His church — "By their fruits you will know them!" You can always tell a member of Christ's church by the kind of production he gets out of his life. If he breeds hatred, if she causes pain, if he wrecks instead of builds, if she ruins reputations instead of helping people — well, take another look. Christ's people are builders. They are like good solid apple trees. They don't just dig in and eat up the food of the soil. They give apples.

The things these Christian people do are not always flashy. In fact, most of the time the real people of Christ do their work quietly and strongly, forgiving each other and even folks who don't like them, trying to get along with kindness in jobs and homes and streets. Well, you won't see them lighting firecrackers to show you how great they are. Christ once sailed into a supposed follower of God for saying his prayer aloud in the temple and thinking himself better than a poor sinner across the way. So if you spot any Christians with proud head and holy-holy eyes, go the other direction. You haven't found a member of Christ's church.

So what you're looking for, if you want to join Christ's people, is the church of those who love Him, who love each other, and who are not proud about any

69

part of it. And, of course, you'll want to join the people who keep their eyes trained on the right historical record of Christ — or you'll end up worshiping some golden calf or other. In other words, you'll want to find a Scripture-loving people, for the Bible record is the only Gospel record we have from the time of the Lord Himself.

Maybe you have a few ideas about joining the right group of people, about finding the one real church.

But this isn't the last of it. Even after you find those people, even after you worship with them, you'll spot plenty of flaws in their character. Nobody is perfect — not even you.

You'll soon see that the church isn't for well people. It's for sick people. It's for people who know they need Christ, because they know that they *do* go against the grain of God by their thoughts, words, and actions.

The church is a very personal thing to these people. They know themselves. They want Christ's healing. They come together to thank Christ for healing them. This amounts to a group activity. And yet the worship and thanksgiving remains a *private* concern between each worshiper and Christ!

Because finally every one of us has to face Christ alone. And every one of us has to become a "church" all by himself. And every one of us has to make a private covenant with the Savior:

"Lord, I want You. Take me in return."

That's what the church is made of — not laws but love. Christ's love for you and your love for Christ.

You're Afraid
to Die

Jesus Christ is just wonderful to know. But you have to know Him to find that out. And you have to be willing to move around to hear Him speak to you — at church, when you are with His people, and when you are at home alone, in the perfect stillness of your own room, reading your Scripture and praying.

One of the reasons Jesus Christ is so wonderful is this: He understands you. He not only loves you, He feels *with* you. He shares your feelings of fear, and love, and desire, and need. He understands your fear of death.

When you read the Gospels of Matthew, Mark, Luke, and John, you'll be surprised at how many times Jesus Christ talked about death — and about life in the face of death. He knew, all right — He knew full well how His own disciples quivered before the grave. Jesus knew how the people who followed Him, hanging on His every word and thought, could not stand to think of the black years of death ahead of them. Jesus wanted to help them — and that's why He talked to them, so often and so powerfully, about dying.

What did He say?

Jesus Christ said: "He that believes in Me shall *never* die!" The Gospel writer John reports those very words in his 11th chapter, the 26th verse.

What nonsense that makes at first hearing! We read about Christians as well as non-Christians dying every day. The death rate in the church is just as high as anywhere else. And Christians seem just as dead as anyone else when they die. How could Christ seriously say what John tells us He said? Or was John trying to create a man of miracles out of a man of straw? Or was Jesus Christ talking just to draw a crowd?

Nothing of the sort. Jesus has been accused of just about everything under the sun — except not meaning what He said. He always meant what He said, and He spoke with force of thunder, "with authority, and not as the scribes!" And since the words and life of Jesus are better recorded than any other fact in history, and since Scripture itself gives every evidence of being inspired by God Himself, we simply have to face up to the words: "He that believes in Me shall never die."

The fact is that Christ knew better than any of us what death really is all about. When He talked about death, He talked about the whole matter of dying physically, *and* the judgment, *and* spending life in either heaven *or hell* for all eternity. "Have no fear of those who kill the body but cannot kill the soul; rather fear Him who can destroy both soul and body in hell!" And when Christ spoke about death, He meant the kind of death which lasts not only a second but all eternity — the kind that hits with the force of a tornado and never lets down. He meant the *spiritual*

74

death which starts here on earth with people who do not love Christ and which goes on and on without end. Christ meant, by death, "being without God"!

But if — and when — you take this Jesus Christ to be your very own Lord and Savior, you are never, never, never without God again. Not now. Not in eternity. So — you just cannot die!

Think a moment. What is death to a Christian? He falls asleep — and wakes up in the presence of the Lord Jesus Christ Himself! You know how it is when you fall asleep at night, how you drift into complete unconsciousness and wake up, seemingly immediately, the next morning. Actually you have slept eight or nine hours. But you can't remember a single one of them.

So is death for the Christian — a sleep of forgetfulness.

Then morning.

Then life forever, right next to the great Lord and Savior, who gave life in the first place — and then, at Calvary, added the capital L to make that read Life!

Do you want this Life for yourself?

Take Christ to yourself, then. And that Life is yours. And you will not die. You will never die. You are forever.

For "Christ has conquered death, and brought Life and immortality to light" — just for you. And in heaven, at the throne of His Father, Christ will greet you as you come to Him.

So beautiful, so real, can this Good Morning expectation grow in you that you will learn to long for that day. So full of wonder can your days even on earth become, because you are with the forgiving Christ, that you will look forward with anticipation to meeting Jesus Christ in all His fullness and glory. So that, sometime in your life here, you will find yourself saying with the writer John in Revelation, the last book of Scripture —

"Amen, Lord Jesus, come!"

This is no dream world. This is fact. This is great. And this — this hoping and longing, waiting for eternity — can make your work and your play and your dating and your every effort a lot more fruitful long before you personally meet Christ.

Try it, and see.

Sailing Out
with Christ

Maybe, by now, you have made a decision to keep on going with Jesus Christ. Here's hoping you have! For you are going to enjoy some of the most sparkling adventures in creation — if you take Christ along in your life.

Life itself is an adventure — and quite a long one, at that. And like any adventure, it has its high points and its low. You want to be prepared for both, don't you?

You want to get yourself set to last the full distance. The long pull is the thing. You don't want a companionship with Christ which will get you all steamed up for only a mile of a hundred-mile haul. You want to know Christ in such a way that you *stay* refreshed and strong in His presence.

Now, how can you get that kind of refreshment and strength?

Almost immediately after Jesus Christ went to His death at Golgotha, and rose again mightily after three days in the grave, those who knew Him best started to write down their memory of what He had said and done.

Among these writers were some of the followers:

John and Mark, Matthew the publican, Luke the physician; and also a man who never met the Lord during His earthly stay but had a special vision of Him on the road to Damascus after Christ's resurrection — Paul of Tarsus, a city up north in Cilicia of Asia Minor, completely out of Palestine.

Why did these people set to work at writing down their knowledge of Jesus Christ?

Sure, they wanted to preserve the history of their Savior's words and acts. Luke, especially, wrote quietly and completely of all his Lord had said and done — and proved to be one of the finest historians of all time.

But there was more on the minds of these writers than just history.

These men wanted to write down words by which other people, in other times, could live through the experiences with Christ which they themselves relished so much!

In other language, they wanted *us* to have a record by which we could ourselves *live with Christ*. They wanted us to refresh ourselves with the presence of our Lord *as we read!*

Think of your New Testament in that light. How much more doesn't it mean to you! This isn't only a bunch of printed facts. This is a way of life.

That's the way you have to read this record of Jesus Christ. This record is the Way He wants to walk with you, and the Way He wants to keep giving you spiritual blood transfusions.

In physical life you may need blood transfusions only once or twice in 70 years. But in spiritual life you need this restrengthening every day. Otherwise you'll start to feel weak, your life with Christ will fade little by little, and you may even drift completely off into a world where you stand altogether alone.

So the thing for you to do, if you want to keep spiritually healthy and robust, is to spend some time each day — if only a few minutes or a quarter hour — in studying a page or two of this record of Jesus Christ which we call the New Testament. And then look into the Old Testament for signs of His coming — for long before the first Christmas in Bethlehem this Old Testament told people He would come to earth visibly!

How the name of *Jesus Christ* rings in your ears long after you have set your Bible aside! How warm and safe and strong you feel after you have tasted His words and His actions in your daily reading session! You can do a lot worse than to keep a pocket New Testament with you always, available for study and thought in out-of-the-way moments and places — on the bus or streetcar, after school, during those ordinarily boring moments at lunch hour, in home-room. . . .

You'll discover a lot of thrilling ideas about your Lord in Scripture.

And — plus that! — you'll learn about:

a) getting together with your fellow Christians in church life

b) joining the congregation of Christians

c) discovering the complete world of Christian doctrine

d) refreshing your life with Christ through the sacraments

e) staying close to your Lord in your daily prayer life.

So — if you are not yet a member of a Christian congregation, start searching right away for that church which talks the full truth of Jesus Christ.

And — if you are already a member of a Christian church, set yourself to explore life with Christ to the fullest. Make this your first love in your world.

The sun rises and sets because Jesus Christ is after your soul. He loves you. He wants you. He is calling out to you. He is reaching out to touch you.

Answer back, will you?

Hold out your hand to His.

Finally...

This little book has tried to say in many ways:

√ *That Jesus Christ is for you*

√ *That you can find Him, and life with Him, in the New Testament Church*

√ *That life with Christ is the happiest, healthiest, most adventurous life there is!*

No matter who you are, age 13 or 19, fellow or girl, hero or waterboy — don't forget. . . .

ASK JESUS CHRIST FOR HIMSELF

This can be the beginning, for you, of a whole new life. Take it. Take Him.

This is *just* the beginning.

And there is no end to Him, to His kind of Life, ever.

From here on, it's God and you, together, forever.

"Ask, and the gift will be yours; seek, and you will find; knock, and the door will open to you." *Matthew 7:7.*